Little Boat

Wesleyan Poetry

LITTLE BOAT

Jean Valentine

Wesleyan University Press

Middletown, Connecticut

Published by Wesleyan University Press,

Middletown, CT 06459

www.wesleyan.edu/wespress

Printed in the United States of America

5 4 3 2 1

Library of Congress Cataloging-in-Publication Data

Valentine, Jean.

Little boat / Jean Valentine.

p. cm. — (Wesleyan poetry)

ISBN-13: 978–0–8195–6850–2 (alk. paper)

ISBN-10: 0–8195–6850–3 (alk. paper)

I. Title.

PS3572.A39L58 2007

811'.54—dc22

2007013487

For
Eleanor Ross Taylor

Contents

Little Boat

La Chalupa, the Boat

I am twenty,
drifting in la chalupa,
the blue boat painted with roses,
white lilies—

No, not drifting, I am poling
my way into my life.   It seems
like another life:

There were the walls of the mind,
There were the cliffs of the mind,
There were the seven deaths,
and the seven bread-offerings—

Still, there was still
the little boat, the chalupa
you built once, slowly, in the yard, after school—

For her

For her,
for the tense mare and her rider
with her harness and blade
with her eyes and hooves straight ahead

with her unit   rising perfect
out of the father-ground   —"ready"—

For her,
once a foal   For her,
born, like many a foal, born with a
wet-black line of hair down her spine—

The Artist in Prison

I will trade
what — cigarettes

for their socks
for threads

to embroider little
pictures for you

2" x 2"

I will trade

what — whole
days when I was free

    red shadow
    on the inside of my skull

for socks
for threads

for Ray Materson

4

In Memory

I was over at your place,
but you weren't there.
The window was covered:
a leafy gold screen,
but it was a gate, locked, double-locked,
and over that, thick double-velvet drapes—
And then, out of the winter blue,
there leapt from branch to branch this

monkey-armed woman.
Jumping on my back,
suffering things. She was
Addiction— I guess,
but life, too,
skating on axes on her frozen sea,
life demanding life!
Flying life,

demanding to not-know,
demanding to know.
You. Did you ever think
you could do something useful?
You know.
Radiant?

But your touch

But your touch was everywhere, Lord
to be accomplished
though no one could see it
A great human thing was being accomplished
:   it drew every last part of him
into you
              :   the lost sailors, diving for mines
off Korea. Every white hair,
black hair, every invisible
threshold, coarse and fine.

The Poet

for Jerry Stern

Hunger of the tongue
of the belly   the throat   even
the mike creaked
—was it hungry too? Was the lamp
wild to shine?

                The little sounds, &
lights, & everything, alive, & veering, *fun!*
the way you tossed your head, like Johnny Cash—

Photographs at her Wake

Two curved tortoise-shell combs
in her hair
no more breathing in & out

Outside   in childhood
a glint of water
green in the limestone

Inside   in marriage
she & John in their lighted room
comb into comb

Can you feel
a hair under a page of the telephone book?
under two pages? under three?

Mattress on the floor:

my protectors blue
Mary   & Gnesh
Overcomer of Obstacles

two incense sticks
standing in the beach sand
in a yogurt cup

the old rug its dirt and fibers   its beauty
waiting   breathing

*

Night: we buried
that book of
like/dislike

Night: we read that beauty
labor of the body
Vincent   beauty from the body spun

Lord of the world!

Lord of the world!   soft
unconditional galaxies,
look at me look at me!   faraway

animal made out of dots
up in the other sky, Woman!   please you
nurse my child, please

nurse my other child.
Rub my hand discovered
caught in the prisoner's hand, rub
with your milk his hand.

The door is fallen down

The door is fallen down
to the house
I used to try & pry open,
in & out,
painfully,
stiff tears.

I sit underneath the cottonwoods—
Friends,
what am I meant to be doing?
Nothing. The door is fallen down
inside my open body
where all the worlds touch.

Door

Door
to the shining endless bridge
100 floors down
I can't drive this car down
No one can drive their car down
But child, they are heavy. The cars,
they will pull us down.

The father was a carrier

The father was a carrier
He had five buckets
How did he carry it all in those five buckets?
And the men on the ship. *They* were all carriers,
heads and backs and shoulders — Lonely, father, little brothers,
husband, I miss you. So. Heavy-laden.

Gray

gray
"the order of the mother"
one degree Fahrenheit

News armature:

Expect sleet or snow   west coming east

> *You may not have wanted to be there*
> *It may have been because of the pain*

helicopter   on your left side
man asleep
child   on your right

Once I was girls and boys

Once I was girls and boys — now

Now who I love are the wild-
worn drifters, not of the town—

cooking their supper out by the side of the road, kisses kisses

          —And one especially, my mother's
father, lost, glare blue and shaved,

at his own work—
unknown—

on your behalf   child, window
staring for you.

The Eleventh Brother (2)

The car you were driving
flew off the bridge, it was drowning.

This was after *The Wild Swans*—
the story where even though you were her favorite

your sister couldn't finish weaving your shirt,
so when you turned back

to a man, one arm stayed a swan's wing.
The car you were driving

flew off the bridge, it was drowning.
This was after *The Wild Swans*,

your sister had finished weaving your other arm,
she dove down to give it to you

through the gray water. You couldn't
take it. You wouldn't.

"Remote Objects of Intense Devotion"

A guy smoking, in his chair
A guy in his car   intensely

in unrequited love   for Eternity
remote

objects
of intense devotion

as long as one remote glistening soul
     so long will I cry it

still forces
hotly or coldly   a child

     so long will I cry it

The first thing

The first thing this guy takes
is happiness
                    The faint light of the stars
                    In spring: leaping!   lambs!

Next thing he takes
is your skin

Where it was, you grow ten more

—A lifetime learning
you could take off your skins
and just talk out of flesh, to flesh

to lamb   to sleep   to wake

That I had treated you badly

That I had treated you badly

Born and bred in The Violents, over and over
set up house with them

That I had been born half-dumb, half-blind,
my dream life more vivid than waking life, still

I remember the long gray wall
where I got out of the car. When I left them.

That I couldn't be friends
if they wouldn't be friends

That you had treated me badly

Little black coats moving away
on the flat bowl of the window, the train

Day & Night

Day & night
in the little house
breath rising, falling,
unreceived . . .

What did I love most in that house? What did you? I loved
the most the early summer mornings, lying, touching, in the
farmer's square bedroom, the window lightening on the left, the
south, the home-made bed,
the beach we had swum for, old, the dog
kissing us —

All around the outside

All around the outside of the room I was given
they were lying, uncovered
in plastic rags, newspaper, rusted tin;

lying right up against the aluminum siding
of the room I'd been given,
as if it gave off warmth, the siding.

Jesus Said,

Jesus said, Split a piece of wood, and I am there.

The Woman's Poem

An imaginary mother,
to know
human love.

Imaginary friends,
monkeys, artists, to
kiss & have fun.

An imaginary husband—
to be happy—
but he was held on an island, for life.

Imaginary
amnesty.

But the real children!

And now you say
*Split a piece of wood,
and I am there.*

And I am there.

Annunciation Poem

—my silky bed for you
in front of the fire,
a cup for your tea

I have set you a place in
side the hollow tree,
a plate for your bread—

I thought I wouldn't find you,
leaf or snow—
Rain light circles in the window, same light

circles the bread,
circles dark hair, your fontanel
—since that second you've been, been the eye of my eye.

The Poet's Poem

I thought my wearing out my shoes on poems
would please you most—
it was you, pleasing *me* most!

Longing to longing
thrown out from the stars

The Teacher's Poem

"If you don't have red, use green."—Picasso

Jesus said, Fix anything—
Your granddaughter's sorrows, no.

My sorrows,
your end of life   sorrows, no.

I couldn't fix: the stovepipe,
get heat.

There was a past life I can't fix,
a future life   "   "   "

Neither the red nor the green.

Death Poem

Jesus said,
You knew me once why will you not know me
You have moved against me
Your whole earth gone
My life no use to you my death equally no

The Afterlife Poem

Jesus said,
But I *am* "alive"!

It's the same material,
but lighter,
summer stuff,

star-coil,
Akhmatova's hair . . .

Strange Lights

Hospital: *far from home*

No time alone   sun   rain
Can't talk, can't see out,
can't even see to any depth down!

What about youth?   Its car?   What about
the bride's foot?   cinnamon slipper—

Now you, Ohio
your winter fields like covers
over me—

Hospital: At last

At last I saw the broad leaf of a flower move, and
underneath I saw a procession of creatures, of the color and size
of green and grey grasshoppers, bearing a body laid out on a rose-
leaf, which they buried with songs, and then disappeared. It was a
fairy funeral. — William Blake

Dearest, what were you doing there tonight?
Where they all understood
everything they said.

You came to make yourself a road
through the house. *A room?* you said,
is it?   *It doesn't measure out.*

A poem?   You cut it into pieces,
slept under it.

Time—you bore it on a green leaf
under the ground.

Hospital: *strange lights*

I needed a friend but
I was in the other room
—not just the other room,
another frame
dragging   blue
or brighter blue: strange lights:

The doctor singing from *The Song of Songs*
'in the secret places of the stairs'

Us standing there   in the past
as we were
in life
you turning and turning my coat buttons

Hospital: It was euphoria

It was euphoria
little veins of it sent

burst to the brain
three little fireworks
white on the gray MRI

it was euphoria

when you stove my boat
& brought me over
listing in the racing foam—

Hospital: *Scraps*

Scraps of hard feelings
left on the floor
winter material

But out the window
sun on the snow
Dressmaker's pins
—somebody's soul
a feminine glint in the trees

A Bowl of Milk

The Look

Pain took me, but
not woke me— no,
years later, your
look
woke me:
each shade & light:

to earth-love then
I came,
the first
beach grasses.

I wanted to be sure to reach you

—But to go away!
And I wanted to be sure to reach you!

And the charge still in us   ankle waist & wrist
& eyes   —Not see you!

Or you to reach me, so
with our townspeople at last we could rest.

But to you now I offer — forgive me, River —
what I could never then, give over.

When she told me

When she told me over the telephone you died
I lay down and cried, "Don't you stop loving me."

In the West Side Market, I heard your voice
from the ceiling say out loud to me, I love you.

In the park, to a chestnut tree,
to the light through hundreds of leaves, I said, I love you.

It *was* you.   And it was my life, run, to what,
—you closer than touch.

This Side

The grave window-eyes across the street
look in, eyes open, half-open,
or gone asleep.   Madonna
Lord.   I wait,
antenna out at an angle,
wrapped with aluminum foil, the radio
 turned this way or that— or the aerial
snaps right off & I carry it with me,
caduceus.

          And I left
a bowl of milk outside the threshold the night
the souls of the dead return, & in the morning
licked it where he licked.

His White Jade Eggs

Is the train I'm on, moving?   or is it
the train next to this one?

It's floaters
                drifting off & up & out of sight,
the whole November city, jazz, the white eggs,

No more those oval in-breaths & out-breaths of his—

I was lying there

I was lying there, half-alive
in a wooden room at a Russian country place.
You sat by me quietly.   It's true you left
sometimes, but came back, sat by me
kindly   quietly.
Woodsman, would you go back to the little-
light-wrapped trees
and turn them on again?
The hide of the deer shivered
The summer wind riffled through my hair.

                                        You are on

a long, patient, summer visit from death.
I am forgiven.   Forgiving.   To your place
the next to be born.

The Harrowing

The worn hands
spines   feet
                    Even he
whose blank hand I held on to
for dear life
                    phantom limb

On your sidewalk
walking past your café

the piano was being tuned, hard,
trying it, one note at a time

trying, walking outside of time
—was that the night—   & space

Blessed are those
who break off from separateness

theirs is wild
heaven.

From the Questions
of Bhanu Kapil

Where did you come from/how did you arrive?

From Tipperary.   In swaddling clothes.

Slowly I followed for the far opening
in the long cloth tunnel

This is what birth was like, I thought—
trying to follow the body

up its stem to the air—
                              I couldn't
find my way out.   Only throw myself out

against the restraining blankets, cold, wet
swaths of home.

What is the shape of your body?

Staunch meadows for the children
reservoir

Reservoir
your thin ghost-body

Whatever kind of eyes
you have now, lend to me—

What do you remember about the earth?

All night long I listened to the coal train,
I whirled, I davened,
I danced, I skipped like the hills,
and I was satisfied.
All night long I lay on my bed,
my throat sang, and I was satisfied.

What are the consequences of silence?

A quilt of mothers and children:
your name embroidered with red thread
in cursive on a white square
against the gray field of the quilt, your
name along one side   your mother's name
—Was she eighteen?   along another side beside
another mother & child of 1922:

Your name & your mother's name, the surname
was made up, an anagram, you told me, years later:
your mother & father
could not marry.   The night I saw the quilt
on my uncle's bed where I slept the night he died,
it was my grandmother's quilt from a church sale,
I was twenty, your student.

I was going to tell you about it, your name, but the air
was too thin, I couldn't.   I wrote you about it,
but you never answered or spoke about it;
two years later, we were in love, and still
never talked about it: not about the quilt, not about
our lips that never touched—

How will you/have you prepare(d) for your death?

quiet   ready
the wires inside the walls

and when no wires
and when no walls

—with you it wasn't flesh & blood, it was under:
I know you brokenheart before this world,
and I know you after.

Maria Gravida,
Mary Expectant

Maria Gravida

Then the gold mother began her touching me
With her long brown face & hands
She tickled me & told me I was beautiful
She held me in the ikon & we gazed

We had a pretty goldfinch   death   salvation
Love was strong as death   Peacocks walked by
Blue immortality   Finches played in black branches
Souls around the cross   It was death in life

Our gold earth gravida
Not a casket but a darkroom for our love
The herma wrought of silver, gilded in fire
Gold mother around me inside me gravida

Eye of water

I have nay ben nn
To keep nn safe
I cannot keep them safe

If nn tway
If nn thee

Keep them
Eye of water

Moose and calf

Moose and calf eat the shoots of the willow trees
along the Alaska highway
looking for you

thirsting after don't know
before I can't remember you any more
Call to me!   friend

whose heart in your side is broken in two
just by a chance comma of time;
still, within the wound in your side

is *a place*
inviting fair—large enough (I saw)
to offer refuge for all.

To my soul (2)

Will I miss you
uncanny other
in the next life?

And you & I, my other, leave
the body, not leave the earth?

And you, a child in a field,
and I, a child on a train, go by, go by,

And what we had
give way like coffee grains
brushed across paper . . .

The Rose

a labyrinth,
as if at its center,
god would be there—
but at the center, only rose,
where rose came from,
where rose grows—
& us, inside of the lips & lips:
the likenesses, the eyes, & the hair,
we are born of,
fed by, & marry with,
only flesh itself, only its passage
—out of where?   to where?

Then god the mother said to Jim, in a dream,
Never mind you, Jim,
come rest again on the country porch of my knees.

Notes

"The Eleventh Brother"

    The Wild Swans is by Hans Christian Andersen.

"Remote Objects of Intense Devotion"

    This is a phrase from the Metropolitan Museum's Surrealist Show, describing work by Joseph Cornell.

"The Woman's Poem"

    "Jesus said, Split a piece of wood, and I am there." From The Gospel of Thomas, in The Nag Hammadi Library, James M. Robinson, General Editor, HarperCollins, 1978, 1988.

"The Teacher's Poem"

    Picasso: hearsay.

"Hospital: *At last*"

    This poem is drawn from "Fairies," an essay in *The Wedding Dress*, by Fanny Howe, University of California Press, 2003.

"I wanted to be sure to reach you"

    This line is from Frank O'Hara's poem "To the Harbormaster."

FROM THE QUESTIONS OF BHANU KAPIL

    These questions are from *The Vertical Interrogation of Strangers* by Bhanu Kapil Rider, Kelsey Street Press, 2002.

"Moose and calf"

    "For there within, he showed a place that was inviting fair; and large enough it was to offer refuge for all" is from *Revelation of Love*, by Julian of Norwich, Image Books, 1997.

"To my soul (2)"

    The last stanza is drawn from the work of Dorota Mytych.

Acknowledgments

Grateful acknowledgment is made to the following periodicals in which poems in *Little Boat* first appeared: *American Poetry Review, Apocryphaltext, Black Clock, Columbia Journal, Columbia Poetry Review, Court Green, crazyhorse, Field, Five AM, Hotel Amerika, Hunger Mountain, Kestrel, Lumina, Lyric,* the *New Yorker* ("To My Soul"), *Octopus, Pleiades, Pool,* and *Salamander*. "The Artist in Prison" was made into a broadside for Kent State University by Eric May. "How will you/ have you prepare(d) for your death?" was made into a broadside for Columbia College Chicago by April Sheridan. The sequence "Strange Lights" was made into a chapbook for The Center for Book Arts (2005) by Roni Gross, with drawings by Peter Schell.

To the editors, and to the Blue Mountain Center, the MacDowell Colony, and the Virginia Center for the Creative Arts, my deep thanks. And I want to thank, for their loving kindness to me and to this book, Kaveh Bassiri, Myra Goldberg, Kate and Max Greenstreet, Joan Larkin, Anne Marie Macari, and Stephanie Smith.

ABOUT THE AUTHOR

Jean Valentine won the Yale Younger Poets Award for her first book, *Dream Barker*, in 1965. She is the author of ten books of poetry, including most recently *The Cradle of the Real Life* (Wesleyan, 2000) and *Door in the Mountain, New and Collected Poems: 1965-2003* (Wesleyan, 2004), which won the National Book Award for poetry in 2004. Valentine has also been the recipient of a Guggenheim Fellowship, a Maurice English Prize, a Sara Teasdale Award, and awards from the National Endowment for the Arts, the Bunting Institute, the Rockefeller Foundation, the New York Council for the Arts, and the American Academy of Arts and Letters.